L
I
F
E

V
I
E
W
S

Published by Creative Education
123 South Broad Street, Mankato, Minnesota 56001
Creative Education is an imprint of The Creative Company

Art direction by Rita Marshall; Production design by The Design Lab/Kathy Petelinsek
Photographs by David Liebman

Library of Congress Cataloging-in-Publication Data

Halfmann, Janet. Life under a stone / by Janet Halfmann; p. cm. — (LifeViews) Includes index
Summary: Examines the nature and behavior of many small creatures, from millipedes to earthworms,
that live in the dark, cool dampness under stones. Suggests several related activities.
ISBN 1-58341-075-9
1. Soil animals—Juvenile literature. [1. Soil animals.] I. Title. II. Series: LifeViews (Mankato, Minn.)
QL110.H25   2000
591.75'7—dc21   99-23824

First Edition

2   4   6   8   9   7   5   3   1

LIFE UNDER A
STONE

JANET HALFMANN

PHOTOGRAPHS BY DAVID LIEBMAN

Most people look at stones as little more than lifeless objects scattered on the ground. But to a variety of tiny creatures making their homes in the earth, life under a stone offers protection against harsh weather and dangerous enemies. Many of the creatures living under stones must keep cool and damp, or they will die. Some, such as **millipedes**, centipedes, and wood lice, hide under stones by day and come out to eat during the cool, moist evening. To avoid enemies, ant mothers crawl under stones to start their **colonies**, and stone fly babies cling to stones to keep from being washed away in fast-running streams. What is life like for the dwellers of this dark, damp, hidden world?

Rocks make sturdy, well-sheltered homes.

Millipedes and centipedes hide under stones by day to avoid the sun. Unlike insects, these many-legged animals, called **myriapods**, can easily dry out because their tiny breathing holes stay open all the time. Most kinds of millipedes are hard and shiny. The millipede's long, worm-like body is divided into ring-like sections and is covered by overlapping plates.

Each body section may have two pairs of short, stubby legs. Millipedes are sometimes called "thousand leggers," though the record number of millipede legs is only 752. Most kinds of millipedes actually have only about 100 legs. A millipede can coil up with its head and legs tucked safely inside to protect itself from danger and to keep from drying out. Many millipedes also ooze liquid from "stink glands" to keep birds and other enemies away.

Most of the 8,000 species, or kinds, of millipedes eat decaying plants, helping to recycle fallen leaves and improve the soil. Being plant-eaters, they won't bite humans or other animals. Millipedes have tiny, simple eyes or no eyes at all. But their short **antennae**, also called feelers, are constantly moving

Centipedes vary greatly in length and color, but all are predators in the chain of life under a stone. They use their long antennae (visible in middle photo) to help find prey.

to explore and find food. Some millipedes are almost too tiny to be seen, while others are more than 12 inches (30 cm) long. Most vary in color from light brown to black. Some species are luminous, meaning they glow like fireflies.

Another insect with many legs is the **centipede**, whose name means "100 feet." Centipedes range in size from 1/10th of an inch (3 mm) to 10 inches (25 cm), and in color from light yellow to a dark or reddish brown. Most species have 30 or 40 legs, but some have up to 354. Centipedes, which have flatter bodies than millipedes, wriggle when they walk or run. They have one pair of legs per segment and use their long legs to chase wood lice, insects, and other prey. Meat-eaters, they capture their meals with a pair of fang-like, poisonous claws developed from their first pair of legs. Some kinds of centipedes may bite people, but they usually don't inject enough poison to cause serious injury.

Some female centipedes lay their eggs one at a time, cover them with soil, and leave. Others lay a batch of eggs and coil around them, keeping them clean and protected. Centipedes

Beetles often lay their eggs underground or beneath a rock. The worm-like larvae of beetles are called grubs. Some types of June beetle grubs take up to five years to mature into adults.

can live up to six years. In the winter, they look for shelter, sometimes entering houses and other buildings.

The **wood louse** is a crustacean whose relatives are water-dwelling crabs and lobsters. The tiny, wingless wood louse also must live in a very moist habitat. It even provides a built-in swimming pool for its offspring. The female deposits 20 or more eggs in a water-filled pouch on her underside. The young stay in their "pool" for about three weeks after hatching; then a slit appears in the pouch and they escape. They are only the size of a pin's head, pearly white with large black eye spots.

Wood lice breathe through **gills** that must stay moist to work. They venture out mostly at night to eat fallen leaves and other decaying plant material. In the winter, they crawl into sheltered cracks and crevices and rest until spring. There are about 3,500 species of wood lice.

The well-known **earthworm** sometimes crawls under a cool, damp stone. It spends most of its time burrowing in the ground as nature's plow, turning and loosening the soil. The

Beetles are one of the most common insects found around the world. They are generally solitary, which means that they live alone. Most types of ground beetles hide during the day and come out only at night.

earthworm eats its way through the soil, digesting the decaying plant and animal material in it and passing out the rest as rich earth called **castings**. At night, the earthworm anchors itself in its burrow and stretches out its front end to drag leaves and other plant material down into the ground.

Earthworms range in size from 1/20th of an inch (1 mm) to 11 feet (3 m) long. There are more than 1,800 species. The common earthworm (*Lumbricus terrestris*), also known as the **night crawler**, is reddish brown and grows to about 10 inches (25 cm).

The earthworm's body is made up of as many as 150 ring-like segments. Four pairs of tiny bristles on all but the first and last segments help the worm move. Earthworms do not have eyes or ears but are sensitive to light, heat, touch, taste, and vibrations. The earthworm breathes through its thin skin, which must stay moist to work. To keep itself wet enough, the earthworm burrows down into muddy soil, sometimes tunneling down eight feet (2.4 m) to find enough moisture.

Every earthworm has body parts that are both male and female, though two worms must mate to produce offspring.

Earthworms can often be seen above ground after a heavy rain.

The eggs develop in the thick band—called a **clitellum**—located on the earthworm's head. This band becomes a **cocoon** that slides over the earthworm's head and into the soil. In two to three weeks, one or more white, threadlike babies hatch. They go right to work, eating and turning the soil. Earthworms can live up to 10 years.

Sometimes a stone is home to an entire family, or colony. One insect that often chooses a stone home to start a colony is the **ant**. In the summer, special winged female ants, called queens, and winged males swarm from their nests and come together in a mating flight. The male soon dies, but the female looks for a safe, sheltered place to dig a nest. Often, she crawls under a stone, where birds and other enemies can't find her. Since the stone absorbs the heat of the sun by day and gives it off slowly at night, her nest will stay an even temperature. After digging her nest in the soil, the mother ant seals the entrance and lays a small batch of eggs.

Eggs hatch into white, worm-like **larvae**, which the queen feeds with saliva and special eggs she lays for food. The larvae

After mating, the earthworm's clitellum forms a cocoon to protect the eggs. Many slugs—a type of snail that has no shell—live under logs or rocks and hide their batches of eggs there (bottom).

grow and molt, or shed their skins, four or five times. Then each larva spins a cocoon around itself. It is now a **pupa**. As it rests, it changes into an adult ant. Soon it will dig a hole in its cocoon and start its life as a worker ant.

Ants are social insects. That means they live and work together in a community. Each ant has a special position called a caste. The three major ant castes are queens, workers, and soldiers. The queen's job is to lay all the eggs for the colony. Most of the ants in a colony are wingless female workers. They take care of the queen, the nest, and new babies. Soldiers are special workers with large heads and extra-strong jaws, which they use to defend the colony.

Of the 9,500 species of ants, some are no bigger than a dot, while others grow to more than one inch (2.5 cm) long. Like all insects, the ant has a three-part body and six legs. Most kinds of ants have eyes, but they don't see very well. They rely on their long, constantly moving antennae to touch, smell, taste, hear, and even "talk" to other ants.

As the colony under the stone grows, the worker ants

Worker ants from different colonies may fight when they meet (top). Ants often fall prey to spiders, such as the wolf spider (left). Spiders also make meals of crickets (middle) and wood lice (right).

expand the nest. They dig a maze of tunnels with many rooms. There is a chamber for the queen, nurseries for the eggs and baby ants, and rooms to store or grow food. Eventually, the nest that started under the stone may include thousands of ants. In the winter, ants move to the deepest part of their nest, where it is warmer.

Most kinds of ants eat dead and decaying plants and animals, but others gather seeds, hunt other animals, or "milk" **aphids** for a sweet, sticky substance called honeydew. Ants have many enemies, including spiders, frogs, birds, and many kinds of insects. They protect themselves by biting, stinging, or spraying poison.

Another insect builds tunnels under stones—but weaves them of silk. Tiny insects called **web spinners** build tunnels using about 200 silk glands in their feet. Even the babies spin silk. The silken tunnels help keep the web spinners from drying out and protect them from ants and other enemies. When in danger, web spinners run rapidly backward into the deeper tunnels of their nests or pretend to be dead.

Moths often seek shelter in the shade beneath stones or logs. To avoid enemies, moths fly mostly at night. Many species also have unique colors and patterns that help them blend in with their surroundings.

Web spinners, also known as embiids, live throughout the warmer parts of the world, including the southern United States. Their slender, yellowish or brownish bodies are about the size of a grain of rice. Males have large eyes and four long, flexible wings. Females have smaller eyes and are wingless. Two short tails act as feeling "eyes" for running backward.

The males fly to new colonies to find mates, then die soon after mating. The female lays clusters of cylinder-shaped eggs along the sides of her tunnel, then watches over them until they hatch into as many as 200 tiny **nymphs**. She continues to care for the nymphs until they can fend for themselves.

Each tunnel houses a mother and her young. Usually several tunnels interlock together and may connect communities with thousands of members. Although web spinners live together in communities and work together to weave the tunnels, they are not social insects like ants. Web spinners stay in their tunnels by day and feed at night on dead and decaying plants. There are 800 species of web spinners.

Another active insect, the **jumping bristletail**, lives under

Many types of lichens (plant-like organisms) grow on rocks. Lichens have no roots and need only water and sunlight to grow. Some species of snails, slugs, and insects rely on lichens as a food source.

piles of stones and in the cracks of rocky cliffs along the seashore. It can jump up to four inches (10 cm) by rapidly snapping its abdomen downward. Like **silverfish**, its basement-dwelling relatives, the jumping bristletail needs to live in moist places. This insect has been on Earth for millions of years; in fact, its ancestors lived long before the dinosaurs. There are 350 species of this brownish, wingless insect, whose slender body measures about one-eighth of an inch (3 mm) long.

Stones in cool, flowing waters attract the **stone fly**. Adult stone flies crawl around on stones and plants near rivers and streams, and their young grow up clinging to stones on the river's bottom.

The more than 2,000 species of stone flies range from 1/10th of an inch (3 mm) to 1.2 inches (3 cm) long and are light green or brown to blend in with their surroundings. Most kinds have two pairs of long wings that fold flat over their back, but they are poor fliers.

As adults, stone flies live only one to three weeks. Some feed on algae, pollen, and bark, but many kinds do not eat at

Salamanders (top) lay their eggs in water but usually live under stones, in caves, or in other dark and moist places. Crayfish, toads, and slugs can also be found under stones near ponds and streams.

all. The adults' most important job during their short lives is to find a mate. The male drums on a hard surface with the tip of his abdomen to attract a female, and she drums back. The two meet and mate, and a while later the female flies over the water and deposits a mass of about 100 eggs, which sink to the stony bottom.

Two to four weeks later, the eggs hatch into nymphs. The nymphs are poor swimmers and cling to the stones around them. Because stone fly nymphs breathe through gills, they need clean, swift-running water that contains a lot of oxygen. Stone fly babies in a stream are a sign that the water is not **polluted**.

Some kinds of stone flies might be better called snow flies. Instead of finding a warm place to sleep for the winter, winter stone flies change from nymphs to adults during the cold winter months and are active in the snow.

Every animal must find the home that suits it best. Even the smallest stone, though lifeless by itself, may support a tiny world beneath it. For many small creatures—whether they crawl, dig, or fly—a stone is that perfect place.

Salamanders prey on worms and many ground-dwelling insects.

KEEPING ROLY-POLY PETS

Wood lice are amazing little creatures that recycle leaves and other plants. They aren't insects, but crustaceans, and they need a moist place to live. They are easy and interesting to raise, usually living a long time.

You Will Need

- Large plastic container and lid with small holes, or wax paper with small holes fastened with a rubber band
- Small plastic container and lid with small holes
- Soil
- Dead leaves
- Water
- Flat stones or small logs
- Paper towels
- Potato, carrot, lettuce
- Apple corer
- Water spray bottle

Catching Wood Lice

The best time to catch wood lice is in late summer or early autumn. You can make a potato trap to catch them. Make a hole lengthwise in the center of a potato with an apple corer. Close one end of the hole with a small piece of potato. Put the trap in a shady place, such as in the garden. Cover the potato with leaves and wait a few days. Wood lice will come and feed inside the potato. To remove them, tap the potato over the small container.

You can also find wood lice outdoors under stones, logs, moist leaves, plant pots, or other objects. Put them in the small container with a damp, slightly crumpled paper towel. Collect 20 to 30 wood lice if you're hoping to raise babies. Be sure to put the stone or log back the way you found it.

Terrarium Home

1. Fill the bottom of the large container with about 5 inches (13 cm) of soil without lumps, and moisten it with water. Check the soil at least once a week, and spray it with water as needed to keep it slightly moist, but not damp or soggy. Don't let the soil dry out, or the wood lice will die.

2. Cover the soil with a layer of crumbly, dead leaves for food. Add more leaves every other week.

3. Put a couple flat stones or small sticks in the container for hiding places.

4. Cover the top of the container with a lid with small holes, or with wax paper with small holes poked in it and secured with a rubber band.

5. Put a tightly-folded, wet paper towel in a corner to give the wood lice water to drink and to add moisture to the air.

6. Place two or three small slices of potato or peelings on the soil for additional food. Wood lice also eat lettuce and thin slices of raw carrot. Add more food every one to two weeks.

7. Put the container in a cool place without too much light and add your wood lice. If your wood lice become crowded as you are raising them, release some where you found them.

By checking on your wood lice often, you'll be able to see how they live. Wood lice grow by shedding or molting their skin, so you may find old skins in the container— if your pets don't eat them first. Females have one to three broods of young per year. If you see tiny white critters in the terrarium, those are the babies. They eat the same food as their parents. Enjoy your roly-poly pets.

CREATE A SHADY LITTLE ZOO

You can attract creatures that like a moist and shady home. Place a fairly large stone, small log, or board on the ground. Try to put it where you can leave it permanently so any creatures you attract can continue to live there.

Leave the stone or board in place for a few days. Then carefully lift it to see what creatures have come. Keep a journal of the animals you see and what they do. Always return the stone or board to the same position when you are done, so you won't disturb your little zoo animals.

TO LEARN MORE ABOUT...

creatures that make their homes in dark, moist areas, you can contact:

Center for Insect Science
Education Outreach
Life Sciences South, Room 225
The University of Arizona
P.O. Box 210106
Tucson, AZ 85721-0106
E-mail: insected@u.arizona.edu
http://insected.arizona.edu

Canadian Museum of Nature
P.O. Box 3443
Station D
Ottawa, Ontario
Canada K1P6P4
http://www.nature.ca/english/infoser.htm

Cincinnati Zoo & Botanical Garden
(Insect World—largest display of live insects in North America)
3400 Vine Street
Cincinnati, OH 45220
http://www.cincyzoo.org/index.htm

Entomological Society of America
9301 Annapolis Road
Lanham, MD 20706-3115
http://www.entsoc.org/

National Institute of Environmental
Health Sciences
P.O. Box 12233
Research Triangle Park, NC 27709
E-mail: sowardm@niehs.nih.gov
http://www.niehs.nih.gov/kids/home.htm

Worm Digest
P.O. Box 544
Eugene, OR 97440-0544
E-mail: mail@wormdigest.org
http://www.wormdigest.org/home.html

Young Entomologists' Society, Inc.
6907 West Grand River Ave.
Lansing, MI 48906-9131
E-mail: YESbugs@aol.com
http://members.aol.com/YESbugs/
    mainmenu.html

INDEX

For many creatures, a stone is the perfect home.